BATS

Printed in China

Library of Congress Cataloging-in-Publication Data
Hutson, Anthony Michael.
Bats / Tony Hutson
       p.   cm. — (WorldLife library)
Includes bibliographical references (p. 72).
ISBN 0-89658-500-X (alk. paper)
 I. Bats **I**. Title. II. Series.
QL737.C5 H82 2000

                                                    00-038181
                                                    CIP

Distributed in Canada by Raincoast Books, 9050 Shaughnessy Street, Vancouver, B.C. V6P 6E5
Published by Voyageur Press, Inc.
123 North Second Street, P. O. Box 338, Stillwater, MN 55082 U.S.A.
651-430-2210, fax 651-430-2211

Educators, fundraisers, premium and gift buyers, publicists and marketing managers: Looking for creative
products and new sales ideas? Voyageur Press books are available at special discounts when purchased in
quantities, and special editions can be created to your specifications. For details contact the marketing
department at 800-888-9653.

Photographs © 2000:

Front Cover © Stephen Dalton / NHPA
Page 1 © Jim Clare, Partridge Films Ltd / Oxford
Scientific Films
Page 4 © Alain Compost / Bruce Coleman Collection
Page 6 © Richard Packwood / Oxford Scientific Films
Page 8 © Partridge Films Ltd / Oxford Scientific Films
Page 9 © Mary Plage / Bruce Coleman Collection
Page 10 © Hans Christoph Kappel / BBC Natural
History Unit
Page 11 © Prestige Pictures / Oxford Scientific Films
Page 12 © Dieter and Mary Plage / Oxford Scientific
Films
Page 13 © Jeff Foott / BBC Natural History Unit
Page 14 © Alain Compost / Bruce Coleman Collection
Page 15 a © Nick Garbutt / Indri Images / Planet Earth
Pictures
Page 15 b © P. & W. Ward / Oxford Scientific Films
Page 15 c © Mike Brown / Oxford Scientific Films
Page 15 d © A. M. Hutson

Page 17 © Dietmar Nill / BBC Natural History Unit
Page 18 © Hans Christoph Kappel / BBC Natural
History Unit
Page 20 © Kim Taylor / Bruce Coleman Collection
Page 23 © Dieter and Mary Plage / Oxford Scientific
Films
Page 24 © Stephen Dalton / NHPA
Page 26 © Dietmar Nill / BBC Natural History Unit
Page 27 © Alastair Shay / Oxford Scientific Films
Page 28 © Stephen Dalton / Oxford Scientific Films
Page 31 © Kim Taylor / Bruce Coleman Collection
Page 32 © Juan Manuel Renjifo / Oxford Scientific Films
Page 35 © John Visser / Bruce Coleman Collection
Page 36 © Jens Rydell / Bruce Coleman Collection
Page 39 © Dietmar Nill / BBC Natural History Unit
Page 40 © Vivek Sinha / Oxford Scientific Films
Page 41 © J. L. G. Grande / Bruce Coleman Collection
Page 42 © Tim Martin / BBC Natural History Unit
Page 43 © Dietmar Nill / BBC Natural History Unit

Page 44 © Jim Clare / BBC Natural History Unit
Page 47 © Phil Savoie / BBC Natural History Unit
Page 49 © Merlin D. Tuttle / Bat Conservation
International
Page 50 © David Lazenby / Planet Earth Pictures
Page 52 © Michael Pitts / Oxford Scientific Films
Page 53 © Hans Christoph Kappel / BBC Natural
History Unit
Page 55 © John Lythgoe / Planet Earth Pictures
Page 56 © Derek Bromhall / Oxford Scientific Films
Page 59 © John Downer / Planet Earth Pictures
Page 60 © Stephen J Krasemann / Bruce Coleman
Collection
Page 61 © Roger Jackman / Oxford Scientific Films
Page 62 © B. Odeur / Still Pictures
Page 63 © Gunter Ziesler / Still Pictures
Page 65 © Nick Gordon / Oxford Scientific Films
Back Cover © Arnold Newman / Still Pictures

Front Cover Photograph: Pipistrelle bat in flight.   Page 1 Photograph: Peter's Epauletted Fruit Bat
Page 4 Photograph: Bats flying at sunset, West Java. Page 56 Photograph: Rousette Fruit Bat.
Back Cover Photograph: Honduran white bats – Costa Rica.

BATS

Tony Hutson

WORLDLIFE
LIBRARY

Voyageur Press

Contents

Introduction

I think the first book on bats that I read was called *The White Lady* by Leonard Dubkin. It was largely a work of fiction, but there wasn't much else around on the subject of bats in the 1950s. Nevertheless, it must have had an effect. Following an interview with the chief of Britain's Nature Conservancy when I was still young, and had not yet seen a bat properly, I was able to visit a priory in Hampshire and see a colony of Daubenton's bats, a bundle of tiny balls of fur with little black eyes.

A few years later I joined in on surveys of underground sites for hibernating bats and I was amazed to find these animals in a mine – they were so cold and still that they could have been dead. They were covered in condensation, and could be there for months, waking now and again, but basically ticking over on energy stored up from an autumn feeding frenzy. On reflection, our behavior was undoubtedly very damaging for the bats. We would visit the sites frequently and examine the bats closely; we did not appreciate that even slight changes in temperature that might be brought about by our presence, or our direct disturbance of the animals themselves, could be causing unscheduled arousals, which might cost the bat over 10 days' supply of stored energy – and the balance between being able to make that stored energy last through the winter or not is pretty fine.

At this time (about 1960) the study of bats in Britain was difficult; few people were interested or had the facilities. In 1963 those that were interested gathered at a workshop (a 'bat camp') at Lord Cranbrook's house (he was at the time a pioneer of mammal research and conservation) and discussed bat work, visited field sites and demonstrated techniques. The most impressive equipment was a large electronic box that could convert the ultrasonic sounds of bats to something we could hear and divide into warbles, tweets, ticks and tocks – this was the prototype of the first commercially available bat detector, which was to revolutionize bat field work, along with the development or increased availability of night viewing apparatus, automatic data loggers, C.C.T.V., miniaturization of radio transmitters and

Water has condensed onto the fur of a Daubenton's bat hibernating in a mine.

a host of other techniques that would make the study of bats much more accessible and, for the most part, much less intrusive. Such studies increasingly demonstrated the interesting aspects of bat biology – and the serious declines that were occurring in many bat populations.

My own interests had become directed to the strange array of bugs that are specialized for living on bats and this gave me the opportunity to see some of the more exotic bat species. On the tiny island of Aldabra in the Indian Ocean, I met my first large flying foxes – a relatively small species with a wingspan of only 3 ft 3 in (1 m) – and a tiny free-tailed bat; both are species that occur on Aldabra alone and were threatened by the proposal to develop an airbase there.

The fisherman bat of Central and South America.

Latin America is the Mecca for every bat worker, and my opportunity came with an expedition to Ecuador to investigate a cave that was reported to have been dug out by aliens from outer space 4000 years ago! Here we discovered a new species of nectar-feeding bat, and among the wide array of other species seen were my first vampire bats, which certainly made an impression. Others have remained favorites ever since, such as the tiny proboscis bat, the fisherman bat and the sword-nosed bats. A few years later, during six weeks in Belize, I searched long and hard for the tent-making bats that I knew were there. Only a few days before I left did I stumble across such a bat tent and then, looking around, they were everywhere – it was just a question of getting that 'search image' right.

That first Daubenton's bat colony is no longer there, but Aldabra is now a World Heritage Site and the importance of the bat diversity in countries like Ecuador and Belize is well recognized. Through the constraints of being mammals that need to fly, bats have a

The Honduran white bat is found through much of Central America. It chews the ribs of the leaves of certain plants, such that the leaf folds to form a tent. They may live here singly or in a small group for about six weeks when they must move and find a fresh leaf.

certain uniformity, but within that, the 1000 species offer an extraordinary variety of form and function. Despite their diversity, bats face common conservation problems throughout the world. Some of these problems are shared with other animals and plants, such as loss or pollution of habitat, particularly woodlands and wetlands, but they also have their own special problems which are mainly associated with their aggregation into roosts in caves, trees or buildings either for breeding purposes or for hibernation. While the early research was perhaps purely to satisfy scientific curiosity, research now is increasingly directed to investigating and contributing to resolving conservation problems. Bats figure more and more in biodiversity conservation strategies, in recognition of their conservation needs and the contribution their diversity can make to environmental monitoring.

The common pipistrelle, widespread in Europe.

A poor public image has not helped; neither have ill-conceived projects for their control where they were perceived to be a problem. In many countries their status has moved from pest to protected species, often with special provisions because of their particular problems, but legislation is not enough. Public awareness and an appreciation of their value to humans and the environment are all-important. A change in attitude develops slowly, but it is certainly true that there are many fewer public inquiries now as to how to get rid of bats. More often the inquiry is about how to maintain a population of bats while carrying out other activities, or even how to encourage bats into, say, crops to improve pollination or to assist in the management of insect pests.

A Daubenton's, or 'water' bat, takes midges from or close to the surface of water.

Origins and Diversity

The earliest fossil bats are from the Eocene period of about 50 to 60 million years ago. There are many good fossils from that period, but all are clearly recognizable as bats and have all the characteristics of modern bats. The origins of bats remain obscure. In the late 1700s Linnaeus, the father of biological classification, placed them next to man. Today, they are still placed between primates (including man) and insectivores (such as hedgehogs and shrews) – a long way from the rodents with which they are allied in many people's minds. Most authorities would suggest that they evolved from some small arboreal insectivores and that the development of gliding mechanisms, or hands modified into fan-like scoops for snatching insects from the air, eventually led to flight.

We now recognize nearly 1000 species of bat, making this order of mammals second only to rodents in number of species; a quarter of all mammals are bats. While the greatest

The Californian leaf-nosed bat breeds in very hot caves.

diversity is clearly in the tropics, bats are found throughout the major land masses except for Antarctica. Their power of flight has enabled them to reach islands and, indeed, they are often the only indigenous mammals on many of them, but they have failed to reach the more remote islands of the South Atlantic and Indian Ocean or Pacific islands east of Samoa. In desert areas their diversity will usually be exceeded by that of rodents, but in tropical forests they may easily outnumber other mammal groups in terms of species diversity.

This colony of Mexican free-tailed bats at Bracken Cave, Texas, may number up to 20 million.

The bat species are organized into two suborders and 18 families. One suborder, the Megachiroptera, contains the single family of Old World fruit bats (Pteropodidae) with about 170 species. This group is so distinct that in the late 1980s a major argument erupted as to whether they should be regarded as true bats at all. It was strongly argued that they had a different origin and that they are, in fact, more closely related to the primates than to the rest of the bats. Fierce debates took place in scientific journals and at meetings such as the International Bat Research Conferences. In recent years the argument has settled down and the general opinion is that all the bats have a common origin – they are monophyletic.

The tube-nosed fruit bat.

The other suborder, the Microchiroptera, includes the remaining 17 families of bats. The scientific names for these suborders may be a little misleading, because although it is true that the 'megabats' include the largest species with the biggest having a wingspan of up to 5 ft 6 in (1.7 m) and a weight of over 3 lb 6 oz (1.5 kg) and the 'microbats' having the smallest species with a wingspan of about 5 in (125 mm) and a weight of about 2 g, there is considerable overlap: the smallest megachiropteran has a wingspan of about 200 mm and a weight of 15 g and the largest microchiropteran has a wingspan of 3 ft 3 in (1 m) and a weight of 6 oz (170 g).

The 17 families of Microchiroptera show a great range of appearance and behavior. The largest family of plain-nosed or vesper bats (Vespertilionidae) is relatively uniform in appearance and provides most of the species found in North America and northern Europe. Other major families are the spear-nosed bats (Phyllostomidae) of Central and South America and extreme southern U.S.A., the leaf-nosed (Hipposideridae) and horseshoe bats (Rhinolophidae) of the Old World, and the sheath-tailed (Emballonuridae) and free-tailed bats (Molossidae) found

The Old World fruit bats, such as Wahlberg's epauletted fruit bat of Africa (above) and the tiny blossom bat of Australia (below right) have large eyes, long thumbs and a claw on the second finger. The mouse-tailed bat (below) and yellow bat (above right) are insectivorous species of Africa's dry lands.

15

throughout the tropics and subtropics. The remaining families are generally rather limited in species and usually in distribution, and have descriptive names such as fisherman bats (Noctilionidae), disc-winged bats (Thyropteridae), sucker-footed bat (Myzopodidae), short-tailed bat (Mystacinidae), mouse-tailed bats (Rhinopomatidae), false vampires (Megadermatidae), Kitti's hog-nosed bat (Craseonycteridae), funnel-eared (Natalidae), smoky (Furipteridae), slit-faced (Nycteridae), and mustached bats (Mormoopidae).

There is an obvious emphasis on faces and tails in these common names and the reasons for that will become clear as we look in more detail at the feeding behavior and other aspects of bat biology. Suffice to say at this stage that the curious and sometimes bizarre (or, to some people, ugly) facial adornments of many bats are related to their special systems of echolocation, which allow them to find their way around in the dark, avoid obstacles and find their favored food. However, nobody has yet explained the reasons for the extraordinary appearance of the wrinkle-faced (or 'old man') bat, or the fact that it has a fold of skin under its chin, which it can pull up to completely cover the folds of its face when it is at rest.

The major diversity is in the tropics and species numbers decline as one heads north or south. Only one species is found north of the Arctic Circle in Europe, and there are none at this latitude in North America. The greatest diversity is in Central and northern South America, with well over 100 species in several countries. There are countries of South-East Asia with about 100 species, but in general the bat fauna of Old World tropical countries are significantly smaller than those of the New World. Naturally, even in the tropics, islands have restricted faunas, but even these may include bats that are found nowhere else. Thus, many Caribbean islands have bat species (and genera) that are not found on the mainland and the same is true of Madagascar and others. One species has colonized the small and remote islands of Hawaii and one the Galapagos Islands. Only two species occur in New Zealand (with one, the short-tailed bat, in a family of its own). The little Polynesian sheath-tailed bat occurs on a range of outer islands of the southwest Pacific, and it occurs further east (to Tonga) than any other microchiropteran – even the large flying foxes only reach that little bit further east to Samoa.

The Jamaican fruit-eating bat has many similarities to the quite unrelated Old World fruit bats.

Flight – The Only Flying Mammals

There are so-called flying squirrels, sugar gliders and the flying lemur, but all these, in truth, can only glide; of all the mammals, bats alone have the power of true controlled and sustained flight.

In bats, the arm bones and, especially, the finger bones are elongated, the thigh bone (femur) is rotated through 180° so that the knees point backwards (or upwards) and the tail may be well developed or short or absent. In all bats the flight membrane is stretched between the fingers, body and hind legs. In most bats it also continues between the legs, but this tail membrane may be absent, may be very extensive, may or may not include all of the tail or may extend beyond the end of the tail. The tail membrane is usually supported by a cartilaginous spur extending from the heel more or less along the edge of the tail membrane towards the tail; this spur is called the calcar. In all bats the thumb is free and carries a claw; in most fruit bats there is also a claw on the next finger.

The flight membrane itself is really an extension of the skin between the bones of the arms and legs and the body. The membrane is flexible and elastic and, although appearing very delicate and often translucent, is surprisingly tough. Small holes or tears will heal quite quickly, but large tears or bone breakages will severely impede or prevent the flight essential to find food and so will normally result in death in the wild, although there are records of bats successfully recovering from major tears or even wing-bone fractures. The membrane itself is well supplied with blood vessels and muscles which give it its structure and flexibility. In most bats the wing membrane extends from the side of the body, in some it arises higher up the back and a number of bar-backed bats are so-called because the naked wing membrane arises from the center of the back.

At rest the wings are folded alongside the body and in a few species there are folds in the skin where the wing tips can be tucked away for extra protection. The wing tips are usually folded up inside the wing and out of harm's way, but in some long-winged species,

The greater mouse-eared bat is one of Europe's largest species, weighing just over an ounce (35 g).

Like the North American big-eared bats, these European brown long-eared bats have broad wings and tail membranes for slow hovering flight, to pick insects off vegetation; their large ears enable them to hear the movements of their insect prey.

there is a double folding of the wings, as in the bent-winged bats.

Wing shape varies according to habitat and foraging behavior. Species such as the long-eared bats of Europe or big-eared bats of North America have relatively short, broad wings and a large tail membrane; maybe even their huge ears, which are nearly as long as the body, contribute to the flight area that keeps them airborne. They can fly very slowly and gently among enclosed vegetation or hover around trees and shrubs or above ground vegetation searching for their insect prey. At the other extreme, free-tailed bats such as the Mexican free-tailed bat, and especially the African Mastiff bat (*Otomops martiensseni*), and its relatives, have very long and narrow wings; they do not have the same maneuverability and so forage in fast flight in the open – they are like the swifts of the bird world. Most of the fruit bats have a relatively slow, flapping flight and can hover to take nectar, flowers or fruit.

Powered flight enables bats to forage over an extensive area in a single night, as much as 38 miles (60 km) from the roost in the case of the Mexican free-tailed bat, before returning at dawn to its daytime roost. It also allows long-range movements to follow changing food supplies or to seek suitable places for hibernation (see Migration). The close relationship between flight morphology and behavior and the echolocation style of particular bat species, and hence the kind of food taken, is increasingly well recognized. The relationship between wing-shape and migration is not so obvious: bats with long narrow wings, such as the free-tailed bats and noctule bats, are good migrators, but then Nathusius's pipistrelle is broader winged and more strongly migratory than its congener the common pipistrelle. Even the long-eared or big-eared bats are perhaps much better at medium- or even long-range movements than we might expect, because long-eared bats are usually the first to find newly created sites, have been found on oil installations or light ships far out in the North Sea and can be found hibernating in remote sites not occupied by other species.

Bats are brilliant at flying, but they are also pretty good at not flying! Most people's idea of a bat at rest is of it hanging by its toes from the roof of a cave or from a branch – and that is exactly what many bats do. As the weight of a bird settles on to its bending knees and ankles, so the tendons tighten its toes to 'lock' it on to its perch. In a similar way, the weight of a bat aligns the legs so that the claws of the feet, which are all identical, are perfectly adjusted to hook on to any irregularity of the roost surface. The bat can hang effortlessly, to the extent that if it were to die while hanging it would continue to hang in the same position it had occupied in life. Of course, not all bats just hang by their toes; many tuck themselves horizontally or vertically into crevices, or have other roosting behaviors that will be discussed later.

Wherever bats roost, in caves, tree-holes, buildings or a variety of other places, they mostly roost off the ground and with the head down. Common questions are, why hang upside down and why doesn't the blood all rush to the head? There are several theories to answer the first question and perhaps the favorite is that the wing structure and loss of weight-carrying capability of the legs would make it difficult to do otherwise, but particularly the bat only needs to drop from its 'perch' to be in flight – it does not have to launch itself into the air and struggle to be airborne. The longer, narrow-winged bats need to drop a greater distance to get their flight under control (a further similarity with swifts), but that is usually not a problem. By roosting from the roof of a cave, say, bats are safer from predators and can escape more readily from threatened predation. As to the question of managing the blood flow, the circulatory system of bats, including its valves and pumps, is essentially the same as ours, and well designed to regulate the flow to stop the blood rushing to a bat's head, in exactly the same way that it prevents our blood from collecting in our feet.

Despite the fact that their knees, and hence feet, face backwards, most bats are quite agile on the ground. Crawling or climbing is greatly helped by the thumb with its well-developed claw. Some, such as horseshoe bats, are not well adapted to crawling, but can do it fairly successfully. The New Zealand short-tailed bat chooses to spend a lot of time on the ground, burrowing around leaf-litter in search of ground-dwelling insects or even ground-flowering plants for which it may be an important pollinator. The most agile bats on the ground are the blood-feeding vampire bats, which can move rapidly in any direction and can leap along or off the ground and into flight with great dexterity. Some bats that can crawl efficiently can have difficulty taking off from the ground, such as those with long narrow wings like free-tailed bats.

Part of a huge colony of Mexican free-tailed bats emerging at dusk.

Echolocation – 'Seeing' in the Dark

The mystery of how bats find their way about in the dark attracted scientists for many years. Even at the end of the eighteenth century, the Italian, Spallanzani, and a few years later the Swiss, Jurine, tried various techniques of investigation; they blinded them, they fitted their ears with little brass tubes, which could be blocked and unblocked. They showed that the eyes were not too important, and that the ears were, but they felt that there must be some sixth sense associated with the wing tips. It was not until 1939, about 20 years after the production of ultrasound by insects had been demonstrated, that Griffin and Galambos, in America, clearly showed how bats use ultrasound to avoid obstacles and locate their insect prey.

Ultrasound is, by definition, sound that is too high-pitched for us to hear. We can hear at best just up to 20 kHz (my own top frequency is less than half that!) and so we can regard ultrasound as sounds above that frequency. We are all familiar with echoes; we might not go around shouting through mountain valleys very often, but are aware, even if subconsciously, of echoes such as the pattern of sound as we drive past a row of parked cars or the struts of a bridge. We cannot build up a very comprehensive picture of our surroundings in this way because the low-frequency sounds that we hear can only return echoes from relatively large objects. It is a feature of sound waves that as the frequency (pitch) of sound increases (rises), the wave length gets shorter and shorter, and so the sound waves will be reflected from smaller and smaller objects. Bats use this principle; they send out a continuous stream of high-pitched sounds and use the echoes to provide them with a 'sound picture' of their surroundings – this is called echolocation. There are extra complications, such as the fact that as sound travels through air, it is degraded (attenuated) and the higher the frequency (the shorter the wavelength), the faster it is degraded. Also, a loud sound can be used in the open to pick up echoes from distant objects, but the use of the same volume of sound within woodland or a cave would produce a confusing array of echoes.

Pipistrelle bats flying in a roof space, emitting their high-pitched echolocation calls.

Apart from the different information that can be retrieved at different frequencies of the sound, the length of the sound pulse and its frequency range are also important. Long sound on one frequency (Constant Frequency or CF) will give different information from a short sound that sweeps down through a range of frequencies (Frequency Modulation or FM). Many bats use one or other, some use a combination of the two. For the identification of individual species there are also variations in pulse repetition rate, rhythm, frequency range, the loudest frequency and the loudness of the call. The pulses that a bat species produces will differ according to its flight style, the habitat it forages in and the kind of prey it seeks. To some extent this helps us to identify the bat species with the use of a bat detector, which converts the original sound into something that we can hear or record.

A Daubenton's bat seeks food near the water surface.

However, the echolocation sounds that bats produce are not like the songs of birds. They have a quite different function and will vary according to habitat and behavior. Thus a bat may chatter quite audibly in the roost before it emerges; when it emerges it will head off purposefully towards its chosen feeding ground; depending on the species, it may feed in the open in the early part of the evening and then move into the cover of woodland to feed; it will search for prey and it will home in on prey it has located; at dawn it will head back home along a well-used route and on arrival back at the roost may circle around the roost entrance with its compatriots before entering the roost for the day. For each of these activities the echolocation calls produced will be varied, although they may still retain some features characteristic of the individual species. Just considering the pulse repetition rate, this may vary from about 12 pulses per second in the search phase, increasing to 25-50 pulses per second having located a potential prey and closing towards it (the approach phase) and increasing to a spectacular 200 pulses per second in the catch or 'terminal' phase (I believe the 'terminal' refers to the end of the call sequence rather than the end of the insect!).

In most species the echolocation calls are emitted through the mouth, in others through the nose and in many cases the facial characteristics are linked to the system of echolocation. The plain-nosed or vesper bats shout through the mouth and the sound is spread out over a wide area; the horseshoe bats call through the nose and the noseleaf is designed to direct the sound to a much more confined area. The chapter on food explains why some of this variation has developed.

The parti-coloured bat of northern Europe.

The development of bat detectors and complex sound analysis programs over the last 40 years have revolutionized the study of bats and given us huge advances in the understanding of bat behavior, capabilities and requirements. The research is also beginning to show us just how sophisticated, variable and 'smart' are the systems used by bats in comparison with our own poor efforts, such as radar.

If you wander around the streets of a north European city such as Copenhagen in a late afternoon in November, you may hear a strange chirping from around the higher buildings. This could be the social call of the male parti-coloured bat trying to attract a mate. Such social calls are quite different from echolocation calls; they are used by a range of bat species and are discussed further in the chapter on breeding.

Food – Bugs, Blossom and Blood

The majority of bats feed on insects and many on huge numbers of them. A tiny 5 g pipistrelle bat is reckoned to eat over 2000 small insects per night. Capture rates of over 1000 mosquitoes per hour are recorded for the northern bat. The Mexican free-tailed bat similarly feeds on prodigious numbers of insects, including many pest species; the 20 million bats occupying Bracken Cave, Texas, eat about 220 tons (225 metric tons) of insects per night. Other species, such as the big- or long-eared bats, take rather fewer relatively large insects.

Each bat species has its own favored foraging habitat, style and food, which will be related to its wing shape, flight style and echolocation pattern. We can classify bats into those that feed in the open, at the edge of woodland or within it. Some species are closely associated with water, others with woodland or pasture. They may take their insects in flight (aerial hawking), by picking the prey off vegetation or the ground (gleaning), by gaffing or trawling insects (or fish) from the water surface, by 'flycatching' (flying out from a regular perch to take passing insects), or by some variation or combination of these. Many of those species that feed on relatively large prey will have a regular feeding 'perch' where collections of the discarded wings and other unwanted parts can tell us much about their diet. But bats are also great opportunists and take advantage of seasonal changes in suitable prey. Thus in the colder temperate areas, in spring bats will feed on almost any insects available, desperate to replace the body reserves they have used during winter hibernation. Later, spring chafers will be the favorite for some species, followed by summer moths and dung beetles, supplemented in autumn by mass emergence of craneflies; seasonal blooms of midges will attract many bats and when the cotton pests are moving the free-tailed bats will be up there after them.

For the most part, prey will be taken by mouth, but often the insect may be scooped up by the wings or tail membrane and passed to the mouth. Similarly, those bats that trawl insects from the water surface may take them with the feet or tail membrane. This might imply that less precision is necessary to catch the prey than if it had to be taken by mouth,

The greater horseshoe bat feeds on relatively large moths and beetles by 'flycatching'.

but one study has shown that in the vast majority of insects that were taken by the wings, the part of the wings that gave the initial encounter was a very small area, so this may not be just a lazy way of catching insects – indeed we all know that you don't swat any more flies by using a larger newspaper! Either way, it is generally felt that it is no good just flying through a swarm of insects with the mouth open – a bat does have to work to take sufficient insects. Thus, those bats that appear to be flying very erratically are actually perfectly in control, but maneuvering constantly in an effort to catch an insect every three or four seconds.

Bats don't have it all their own way. There are many insects that have 'ears' (tympani) that can detect an approaching bat; the insect may start to fly erratically or drop to the ground. There are other insects that respond to any approaching bat by screeching back at it. There is still debate about whether this is a warning that the insect is distasteful (such as in many of the arctiid moths – in which case there are cheats, or mimics, which respond in the same way but are perfectly edible) or that the response may shock the bat or momentarily jam its echolocation system enough to allow an escape. Of course, some bats have an answer for that too; they have extremely quiet echolocation calls or may switch off altogether while hovering and listening for the movements of the prey or for the sounds that it is producing. Thus these 'whispering' bats can sneak up undetected even on insects with good hearing. This 'arms race' of the bats' continual battle to get enough insects and the insects' efforts not to become bat food has many strands. The echolocation frequencies of many bats are concentrated into a fairly narrow (sometimes very narrow) frequency band. The hearing of moths is similarly best within certain frequencies. The bats will benefit from using frequencies that the insects cannot hear and the insects will benefit from being able to hear the frequencies that bats use; there is evidence with certain bats and certain insects of continual efforts to 'outsmart' each other.

I have used the term 'insect' rather loosely; many bats include spiders in their diet; in fact the Australian woolly bat can be said to be a spider specialist. Millipedes and centipedes are also taken, and a few species, such as the pallid bat of North and Central American arid

Long-eared bats are 'whispering bats' and can approach prey unsuspected.

zones, consider scorpions good eating. A few of the larger species of bats of the families of Old World leaf-nosed or horseshoe bats and slit-faced bats, which feed on larger mainly terrestrial invertebrates, will occasionally take small vertebrates. Other bats, the false vampire bats of the Old World and a group of spear-nosed bats of Latin America, are more specialist carnivores, taking small lizards, birds and mammals (including bats) as a regular part

The frog-eating or 'fringe-lipped' bat.

of their diet. The frog-eating bat of Latin America can pick and choose its prey and sneak up unsuspected on frogs that are singing to attract a mate – as with some of the katydids and grasshoppers there can be a cost to being the best singer on the block.

There is one remarkable specialist fish-feeding bat, the fisherman bat of Latin America, with its long legs and tail membrane and huge feet with enormous claws. Flying over fairly still waters of rivers, lakes and even sheltered coastal sea waters, it can detect the ripples of fish at the water surface and gaff them with its feet.

It is a large bat with a wingspan of close to 3 ft (1 meter), its wings set high on its back, very short almost curly hair, and heavy drooping jowls that give it its alternative common name, the bulldog bat. Quite unrelated are the small mouse-eared bats (genus *Myotis*), which include a number of species with large feet and which have been recorded taking fish in a similar way to the fisherman bat. Indeed, one of these species from Mexico must be a fish specialist, with its feet designed almost identically to those of the fisherman bat.

Three species of bat in Latin America feed on blood – the vampire bats. They belong to the family of spear-nosed bats but, curiously, seem more closely allied to the fruit- and flower-feeding end of the family than to the carnivores. The common vampire is widespread and has obviously benefited from the spread of cattle, horses and other larger mammals. Occasional attacks on humans, but more particularly the effect of their regular feeding on cattle, including blood loss and the opportunities the bites leave for infestation by insects such as screw-worm, or for the introduction of disease (including incidents of vampire-bat-related rabies), result in considerable interest from a public or animal health point of view. The other two vampire bat species, the hairy-legged and white-winged vampire bats, are much less common and less well studied because they feed largely on other mammals and birds and have little impact on man and his domesticated animals.

Their feeding on blood, and the myths that have developed around that, may seem unpleasant, but these bats are actually quite remarkable animals. They are not large (the common vampire generally weighs about one and a half ounces – 40 g), but they have a suite of extraordinary adaptions for their way of life. Their maneuverability on the ground is far superior to that of any other bat, their stealth in feeding, their breeding cycle, mutual feeding and grooming and other specializms associated with blood-feeding make them truly fascinating species. I cannot say that I find them attractive and their 'athletic' capabilities make them unnerving animals to handle, but they are amazing creatures and should not be dismissed so lightly because of an 'unsavoury' feeding habit. One vampire bat story concerns the white-winged vampire bat, which feeds largely on chickens as they roost on branches at night: if the attentions of the bat start to awaken the hen, the bat may nuzzle up under the chicken and chirp like a chick until the hen settles again.

As will be apparent from the above, the family of spear-nosed bats of Latin America includes insectivores, carnivores, blood-feeders and fruit- and flower-feeders. No other bat family displays such diversity. In the Old World the only bats to feed on fruit and flowers are the species of 'megabats'. This family is quite distinct from all other bats and it has been suggested that it is more closely related to the primates. Nevertheless, many of the physical and behavioral characteristics and the interrelationships with plants of these two quite unrelated groups of bats are so similar that they provide a wonderful example of 'convergent evolution'. Both groups are very important, in some cases 'keystone' species, for the pollination and seed-dispersal of a wide range of plants. The Old World fruit bats have very little or no tail and tail membrane, they have large eyes, they have no sophisticated system of echolocation and the specialist nectarivores have an elongated muzzle with an extraordinarily long tongue, tipped with papillae to help lap up the nectar. Not only do we see marked trends in the same direction, indeed sometimes to greater extremes, in the New World fruit- and flower-feeding spear-nosed bats, but we also find the same characteristics of bat-pollinated flowers and some of the same adaptations for seed dispersal in plants throughout the tropics and subtropics occupied by these bats. The bat-pollinated flowers may be large and white, open at night, are found at the extremity of branches or on bare trunks (where the bats can readily get to them), they may have particularly strong smells and produce large quantities of pollen or copious nectar; sometimes the pollination is reliant on a particular type of bat putting its head into a precisely shaped flower to ensure pollen transfer to the female stigma. This remarkable adaptation of plants for bat pollination is called chiropterophily. Bat-dispersed fruits are often fleshy and sweet, again positioned where the bats can easily reach them; they may be single-seeded fruits in which the seeds are discarded after the flesh has been eaten, or may contain many tiny seeds that are either passed unharmed or whose germination may be enhanced by passing through the bat's alimentary system. Bats defecate in flight rather more than birds and so are believed to be better at distributing these seeds and particularly important in providing the pioneer plants to recolonize cleared ground.

In comparison with birds, bats have the night sky almost to themselves, while birds have the day. The bats have had to develop special strategies to cope with their night life, but have nevertheless been able to take advantage of most of the food sources used by birds. There are no 'grazing' bats, but some of the fruit-feeders also eat leaves; there are few 'bats of prey' and no truly aquatic bats. There is one Galapagos finch that feeds on blood taken from the developing feathers of boobies, and oxpeckers sometimes take blood, but bats probably excel in the ability to catch insects, in some of the interactions with plants and certainly in the extreme adaptation of the blood-feeding vampire bats.

The straw-coloured fruit bat feeds on a wide variety of fruits and flowers in Africa.

Roosts – At Home With Your Friends

Caves are home to a great range of bat species and many of them are totally reliant on caves or cave-like places (including mines and other artificial underground habitats). Tree hollows also provide natural roost sites for a wide variety of species and both cave bats and tree bats have adopted buildings or other artificial structures, such as bridges. In temperate areas, bats may change from one type of roost site used during the summer for breeding to another type used in winter for hibernation. In the tropics a range of other sites are used, such as under loose bark of trees, among foliage, in the buttresses of large old trees, or in the homes built by other animals; just a few species build a home of their own.

The largest aggregations of bats are found in caves and when the 20 million female Mexican free-tailed bats that occupy Bracken Cave, Texas, each produce their single young, the colony will have grown to closer to 40 million. Breeding colonies of over a million are found in various parts of the tropics and are mostly of free-tailed bats, which fly high and fast and so can more easily spread out over a wide area to forage for insects. Even the large fruit bats sometimes form very large colonies and somewhere between one and two million straw-coloured fruit bats collect seasonally in a forest in Zambia. The evening dispersal of one of these large colonies can be a spectacular sight – the emergence of huge numbers of free-tailed bats is like a plume of smoke coming out of the cave, whirling around in the sky and drifting off to the horizon. These emergences are a tourist wildlife attraction in various parts of the world, where a large colony of bats may take over an hour to emerge. Equally spectacular, but generally only observed by the enthusiast, is the dawn return, when bats collect overhead and stream down into the cave at great speed. At these times, particular birds of prey (including specialist bat hawks) wait around the entrance to pick off individuals from the swarm. Within the entrance, certain snake or even frog species may wait to take their opportunities too, but there is some safety in numbers and certainly none of these predators can take enough bats to have a significant effect on their populations.

In summer, Mexican free-tailed bats may form colonies of millions in caves in the U.S.A.

Constitution Bridge at Austin, Texas, also attracts about one million free-tailed bats, and provides an evening spectacle, but generally numbers of bats in human structures are much lower. In houses, bats may form colonies of up to a thousand, but this is exceptional. Some species move their colony from house to house quite frequently and this may be an inheritance of an original tree-roosting habit, because most tree-dwelling colonies shift roost sites every few days, although the reasons for this are not clear. In houses, bats may be found in the roof space, but equally may only occur around the outside, under hanging tiles or wooden cladding or under the eaves. In the roof space they may be grouped in the open in a warm spot such as at the roof apex or around a heated chimney, or they may be tucked away in crevices, such as those provided by the large timbers of older buildings.

Bats that live in tree hollows probably have little preference for particular tree species, except that certain tree species tend to produce more cavities than others and there may be special requirements of the kind of cavity produced. In the tropics bats frequently occupy the hollows formed at the base of an old tree, but this is rarely used in temperate areas, where bats will tend to adopt hollows formed higher up in the tree, using a natural cavity formed by rot or breaks, especially in over-mature trees or snags, or in the cavities produced by other animals such as woodpeckers.

Cavities under bark or clumps of hanging dead foliage can only provide cover for individual or small groups of bats, but although one thinks of bats hiding in the dark during the day, there are species that roost in the open. The white-lined sheath-tailed bats of Latin America frequently roost in small groups (a harem) on the trunk of a tree, but generally in a shaded area between large root buttresses. Their close relative, the proboscis bat, forms similar groups lined up on the underside of bare branches overhanging a river; this tiny bat has rather grizzled green fur with irregular pale lines on the back and roosts in such a position that it looks like a lump of lichen or a dead leaf. The African yellow bat is colored as its name suggests and hangs in fairly exposed situations in trees and bushes looking like a ripe fruit. A small number of the Old World fruit bats roost in caves, but most in vegetation, some singly or in small groups, the larger species particularly forming large and noisy colonies in trees where they roost in full sunlight and may be active for much of the day.

The long-tongued bat is widespread from northern Mexico to northern Argentina. With its long nose and even longer tongue, it is an important pollinator, but also eats fruit, flowers and some insects. Roost sites include caves, buildings, under bridges and in tree hollows.

Indian flying foxes form large colonies in the tops of tall trees. Somehow most of them seem to sleep in the heat of the day and they will disperse over a wide area to feed at night.

It was interesting to watch a school party being taken through a colony of spectacled flying foxes in Australia: none of the children seemed to be filling in their questionnaires, their clip-boards were on their heads as defense from the occasional 'rain' from the bats above!

Two other families have special adaptations to enable them to roost in vegetation. The sucker-footed bat of Madagascar has an adhesive pad on its ankles, and the disc-winged bats (three species) of Latin America also have a pad on the wrist. Both these bats roost singly or in very small groups in the young rolled-up leaves of certain palms, Heliconia, banana or similar plants. As soon as the leaf begins to open out they must move on to find a new roost.

A European greater horseshoe bat.

All these bats do nothing to their roost site; they have chosen the site because it already provides the conditions they want. This may also be true of most of the woolly bats of Africa through to Australia that occupy the old hanging nests of birds such as weaver birds, sunbirds or scrubwrens, or the species of round-eared bats (*Tonatia*) of Latin America that occupy disused termite nests, but it may be that the bats must enlarge the entrance to the termite nest or manufacture their own entrance into a weaver-bird nest. There are a few records of woolly bats in Africa roosting behind an active wasps' nest inside a disused weaver-bird nest – an apparently risky way of gaining extra protection from potential predators.

A small number of bat species actually modify vegetation to create a home. These are the so-called 'tent-making' bats. In the New World tropics, a few of the smaller fruit-feeding spear-nosed bats will chew the ribs of larger leaves, especially of particular palms, banana or Heliconia, such that the sides or ends of the leaves collapse to form a tent. These may provide a home for up to six weeks before the bats must find a fresh leaf. The different tent-making bats may be quite specific about their choice of host plant and the way the leaf is cut to form the tent. Less ingenious are the tents made by other species, including some larger ones, where they just remove the inner leaves from a bunch of hanging dead leaves so that the outer dead leaves form a weather-proof cover. A more extreme version of this kind of tent is formed by the short-nosed fruit bat of India, which removes small twigs and leaves from the dense vegetation of certain vines or figs to provide a vertical covered chamber in which to roost.

The Honduran white bat rests under a leaf.

We have seen that some bats have very temporary shelter, or no shelter at all, while others are extremely faithful to particular sites, be they caves, tree holes or, for the larger fruit bats, just hanging in trees; even though these regularly used sites may only be used seasonally. Related to this is the extraordinary array of insects and other arthropods that are associated with bats in those sites that are used habitually, even if seasonally; whereas those bats that live a solitary and nomadic existence in temporary open accommodation have more or less no such associated fauna. These associated animals may live in the accumulated guano below the roosts or spend at least a part of their life on the bats. Some are parasitic, some are not, and some we don't know about, but many display the most wonderful specializms to cope with the comings and goings of the bats, on a daily or seasonal basis, or to avoid being removed during the intensive grooming activity undertaken by the bat.

Like the Honduran white bat, these tent-building bats modify a growing leaf to form a tent.

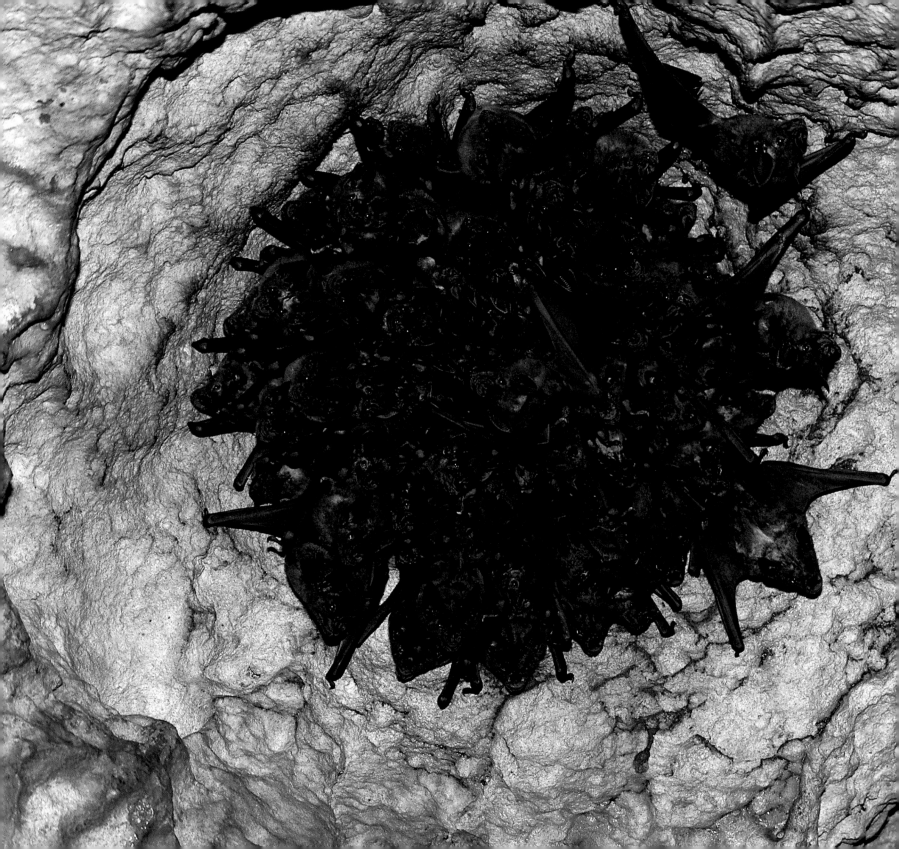

Breeding

Linnaeus, the father of modern scientific classification, placed bats next to primates, largely on the basis that female bats have one pair of thoracic breasts, and on the similarity of the male genitalia of bats to that of primates. Unlike many primates, bats are rarely family animals; the male does not assist in raising the young or looking after the female. Animals can produce a large number of young and trust that enough will survive to replace their parents; a strategy used by most small mammals, including most rodents. Bats are small mammals, but are not 'mice with wings', and have adopted the alternative strategy of producing usually one young (at a relatively advanced state of development) per year, or less often, and trying to ensure that that youngster stands a good chance of survival to adulthood – again, more like primates. Although bats may take a year or two to mature, they can live for over 30 years; remarkable for such small mammals.

For the most part, mating in bats is seasonal. In colder temperate regions, the principal mating period is fall, prior to hibernation. A male will adopt a mating roost and associated territory and attract females for mating. He may proclaim his territory by calling from the roost and in flight, and in some species groups of males will aggregate in the same area, each with his own territory. Individual females may stay with the male for a few days, but through the mating period a successful male will mate with a succession of females. In some groups, e.g. horseshoe bats, mating may leave a vaginal plug that would prevent further matings, but this is not always effective because it can be rejected and the female mate again. In cold temperate climates, fall seems a good time to mate; the male has the summer to set up his territory and ensure that he is in a good condition to attract females, the females have reared their young and are ready to start again, and even some of the females of the year may be mature enough by then for mating. Spring would not be a good time for mating, because all bats arouse from winter hibernation in desperate need to replace the stored energy they have used up. That leaves the females with the problem of not wanting

Greater spear-nosed bats usually live in small groups of one dominant male with females.

pregnancy to proceed through the winter. This is answered by delayed fertilization, a feature unique in mammals; the female stores the sperm and undergoes fertilization in spring. In warmer temperate areas a different strategy, delayed implantation, may occur. Here, fertilization takes place at the time of mating, but embryo development is delayed until spring. In the tropics, fertilization and development of the embryo happen normally, following mating. Curiously, one species, Schreiber's bent-winged bat, demonstrates all three mechanisms in various parts of its range from relatively cold temperate areas to the tropics.

The grouping of males into a display to attract females is best exemplified in birds such as grouse or manakins. In Europe, the noctule bat does essentially the same thing, males collecting into a small area and calling from their individual roosts or in flight. The females might be from local maternity colonies, on migration, or the mating site might be at the end of a migration remote from the maternity site. Similarly, in the Indiana bat of North America, the males collect at a few caves early in the fall and the females migrate to congregate there later. In Africa, the hammer-headed fruit bat has an extraordinarily developed muzzle with greatly enlarged nasal chambers and it produces a loud and resonant 'honk' to attract females. Here, too, the males collect together in a display 'lek'. Its relatives, the epauletted fruit bats, have a more 'refined' call to attract females. On approach by the female the male everts a sac of glandular hairs and flaps its wings to disperse what is presumably a very attractive odor. In this species the glands are on the shoulders, as they are with some Latin American spear-nosed bats; in other groups such glands may be under the chin, on top of the head or on the wings. In the white-lined sheath-tailed bats of Latin America the wing glands may be more to maintain the harem than to attract mates: the male frequently hovers in front of his group of females and gives them a gentle spray with his scent. In this species the male maintains a small harem of females and so do many spear-nosed bats. Subdominant or immature males will roost near the group, but stand little chance of mating until the demise of the older male.

Once pregnancy has started, the fetus develops to a relatively advanced stage by the time it is born. Gestation varies depending on the species and can last from anything between six weeks and four months, or even longer in vampire bats. In pregnancy, the mother may put on

The upper of these Latin American greater fruit bats has a youngster attached. The baby, sometimes called 'pup', in this species is born with eyes open and some hair on the back. It quickly attaches itself to the mother's nipple. It will normally be left behind at the roost when its mother goes off to feed at night. She may return during the night to suckle it. The youngster will be fully grown at about two months old. In Central America this species has an unusual breeding cycle in that the female regularly produces a baby twice per year. The first pregnancy proceeds normally and lasts about three and a half to four months; the second pregnancy takes longer due to delayed implantation of the embryo. Pregnancy is carefully timed so that the young reach independence at the two periods of maximum food availability.

more than a third of her normal body weight. Nevertheless it will be some weeks before the young can fly and anything from six weeks in small insectivorous bats to nine months in vampire bats before the young are independent. Before the young can fly, they are usually left in the roost in a crèche when the mothers go out to feed, but, particularly in the early days, the mothers may return at times through the night to suckle the young. Most bats have only one young, but twins are common in a few north temperate species and some tropical species. The presence of four nipples in the parti-coloured bat in Europe and the hoary and red bats of North America suggest a greater number of young; indeed the latter has been found with three or four babies (or 'pups'). The mothers must produce a large quantity of rich milk and this places a great strain on them. If conditions are bad, pregnant female bats can slow down pregnancy by having periods of torpor, but once born the young must continue to develop. In any case, particularly in temperate areas, it is important that the young are born as early as possible and are weaned quickly because this gives them a much better chance of surviving their first winter. But there will be occasional summers when the conditions are such that the mothers cannot cope and will abandon their young to save themselves for a better chance next year.

In general, then, mating is promiscuous and males play no part in the rearing of the young; the females give birth to one young per year and perhaps not every year in many species; females may have to abandon their young in bad weather and in any case juvenile mortality can be as high as 50 per cent in the first year. Thus, bats breed very slowly and it can take a very long time to recover from population crashes.

Bats are a large and diverse group of mammals and so there are many exceptions to the norm. In vampire bats pregnancy may last about seven months and the period from birth to weaning can be another nine months. These remarkable animals also have one other strategy that is not seen in other bats. A vampire bat mother that has not been able to feed for a few days will beg a feed by regurgitation from a successful female in the colony. But the giving is not altruism; woe betide the well-fed female that does not share her food with a starving roostmate – she will not get fed when it comes to her lean period.

The North American red bat is unusual in regularly giving birth to two or more young at one time.

Migration and Hibernation

Many bat species migrate in response to changes in food supply. We have already seen how the flower- and fruit-feeding bats of the Old World tropics are so closely similar to the quite unrelated fruit- and flower-feeders of the New World family of spear-nosed bats. Alike in form and function, many species of both groups undertake lengthy migrations to follow 'flowering corridors' of their chosen food plants. In Central America, nectivorous long-nosed bats move from Mexico up into the southern states of the U.S.A. along specific routes to take advantage of the succession of flowering food plants. The migration may vary from year to year depending both on the variation in availability of food in Mexico and the success of the flowering of plants along the migration routes. In fact, in this group of bats it is mainly the females and their young that move north while the males remain in the breeding areas of Mexico. In Australia, the flying fox follows the succession of flowering and fruiting trees south into New South Wales and Victoria, but again the southern limits of migration may be dictated for any particular year by the changing success of key flowering trees. In Africa, the straw-coloured fruit bat appears only at the northern and southern limits of its range seasonally, while the large breeding colonies in some areas, such as the colony of up to two million in Zambia, are strictly seasonal in occurrence. In southern South America, there is similar movement, particularly of nectar feeders, in response to seasonal changes in flowering of food plants, but there is also limited evidence of altitudinal movements and this is likely to be an important feature elsewhere.

The migrations or more irregular opportunistic movements of fruit- and flower-feeding bats are essential to them because they have no alternative strategy to cope with local seasonal lack of available food sources. The insectivorous bats of temperate areas also face severe depletion of their food supply in winter. Some species, such as the red and hoary bats of North America, migrate south to continue to feed. Some populations of Mexican free-tailed bats migrate from the U.S.A. to Mexico in winter, but others do not. But most

Some flying foxes undertake seasonal movements to follow the succession of flowering and fruiting trees.

insectivorous bats of these areas have adopted hibernation as a means of coping with the winter shortages of insects. While there is limited understanding of movements to hibernation sites in South Africa and southern Australia, the activity in Europe and North America is better understood. Some species, such as the lesser horseshoe bat of Europe, may move very little distance to their preferred hibernation site. Such species are regarded as non-migratory or 'sedentary', even though some regularly move up to 60 miles (100 km), with many of these journeys taking them across national boundaries. Other species, such as the pond bat and

Schreiber's bent-winged bat is found from Europe to Australia.

Schreiber's bent-winged bat of Europe, will regularly move distances of up to 180 miles (300 km) to suitable hibernation sites and will have regular stopping-off points along the way. These movements will not always be to the south, but in almost any direction to a suitable hibernation site.

The long-range migrants of Europe, such as Nathusius's pipistrelle and noctule bats, which both regularly travel distances of between 930 and 1250 miles (1500 and 2000 km), and the North American gray bat and Indiana bats, are migratory from where there would seem to be a lack of suitable hibernation sites to areas where they can hibernate successfully. Again, in some species the females and their young may be more migratory than the males: in other words, for these species the females move to occupy areas that are suitable for summer feeding and maternity, but have to retreat from those areas in winter. In some species, such as the Indiana and gray bats of North America, the hibernation sites are so specific that in winter most of the population is concentrated in a very few sites; in the case of the Indiana bat, 85 per cent of the known population hibernates in seven caves, or 50 per cent in two caves, and in the gray bats 95 per

The European lesser horseshoe bat is regarded as non-migratory. It might only move from the attic space of a building used in summer to the cellar of the same building in winter, or more usually to a cave or other underground habitat quite close to the summer roost. It may share this winter quarters, its hibernaculum, with other bat species which may have migrated over long distances. Certain sites can be key sites for both large numbers of bats and a range of species, often from a wide geographical area. This concentration of bats into a few key places makes populations very vulnerable to disturbance or to loss of their sites due to closure or change of use.

These bats seek cold and humid environments for hibernation, where they can drop their body temperature to that of their surroundings, slow down all bodily functions and eke out the winter periods, when there is a shortage of their insect food, by using reserves of fat stored up in the fall. Requirements vary according to species, sex, age, condition of the bat and the time of winter. They will wake up from time to time and move site, but unscheduled arousals can be very costly of their stored energy.

cent in nine caves. In Europe hibernation sites holding up to 100,000 bats are recorded (although nowadays, one site of up to 30,000 and one of up to 70,000 are regarded as extremes), but in North America such concentrations are more frequent and up to one million bats are recorded in some mines and caves. Even in these long-range migrants, the movements may not be north to south or the migration routes as concentrated as for many birds: a large-scale banding program in the Baltic state of Latvia demonstrated a migration spread from a little east of South to almost due west to the Netherlands and northern France.

In the absence of the general large-scale banding programs that have been carried out on birds, details of the speed of migrations, the routes followed and many other aspects of migration in bats is rather poorly known. Such banding programs are not generally regarded as appropriate for most species, because recoveries from the general public are few and the data are reliant on specialists searching for marked individuals in summer or winter quarters. These days there is increased emphasis on the employment of other techniques, such as the investigation of D.N.A. to assess the origin of migrants, or the use of modern developments of radar to track movements of migratory populations. Developments in the production of ever smaller transmitters that can be used for the satellite tracking of animals now offer the opportunity to follow the movements of some of the larger fruit bats, but whether this will ever be possible for most of the smaller bats, especially those that roost in underground habitats, remains to be seen.

With the tremendous advances seen in recent years in the understanding of the breeding biology, hibernation and echolocation behavior of bats, perhaps the understanding of migration patterns is the major challenge for the future; certainly the knowledge currently available for a few species and the knowledge that a wide range of species are seasonally absent from known areas suggest that the phenomenon is widespread and an important aspect of the understanding of bat biology and conservation. The fact that only a part of the population of a species may be migratory (particular geographical populations), or that migration is mainly of particular age or sex of a population, is an added complication.

The European noctule bat migrates up to 1250 miles (2000 km) between winter and summer quarters.

Bats and Humans

It is strange that we humans have probably least respect for those animals to which we are most closely related. Primates, particularly apes, have been the subject of fear, ridicule and abuse for centuries. Bats produce a dichotomy of attitude between those who like (or even love) and those who loathe. Both attitudes are probably based on a lack of understanding, those who like them basing their opinion in part on the mystery of bats, which is fortunately only enhanced by having some of that mystery explained. For those who loathe – and they undoubtedly outnumber the others – it seemed a hopeless task, particularly in North America and Europe, to dissuade them of their opinion, but publicity and education have been very rewarding.

Presumably we have lived with bats since we occupied caves and other similar places. As we moved into artificial caves (houses), many bats moved with us. As we removed the larger trees to take wood into our homes, some of those tree-dwelling bats that were losing their homes followed. But there was little understanding as to why bats become so closely associated with humans and there was perhaps some feeling that they were 'after something' or that they had some 'special powers' or influence on our lives. This close association, coupled with a lack of knowledge, has led to misunderstanding, fear and prejudice.

One characteristic of many cultures has been the uncertainty of the nature of bats: are they mammals or birds? A common thread of folklore from around the world centers on this. In competitions between birds and mammals, bats would choose sides to ensure they were on the winning side (a questionably admirable characteristic!), but would sometimes find they had burnt their boats by, say, giving strong allegiance to birds that eventually lost the competition, leading to mammals refusing them readmission and banishing them. This theme occurs in stories from the South West Pacific islands through Asia and Africa to the American Indians.

Such uncertainty may result in suspicion and fear. Hence at one extreme, the Mayan god Camazotz was to be feared and, in the image of a spear-nosed bat, was responsible for monstrous bloody sacrifices. In total contrast is the Chinese approach, where the word for

Rousette fruit bats are among the few cave-dwelling Old World fruit bats.

bat is 'fu' which also means the five great happinesses (health, wealth, long life, good luck and a desire for virtue) and hence the image of five bats appears as a good luck symbol in many circumstances. In-between are the suspicions that resulted, for example, in European farmers nailing a (usually live) bat to the barn door to keep away evil spirits.

Similar divisions have occurred in art, where many have portrayed demons and dragons with bat-like wings, while others have used bats as suggestive of a balmy night. In poetry in England note the stark contrast between 'The Bat' by D.H. Lawrence and 'The Bat' by Ruth Pitter. Bats appear even in philosophy, such as in Thomas Nagel's 'What is it like to be a bat?'.

Bats have been seen as useful in many ways. At times their role in insect management has been perceived as beneficial, and the construction of bat boxes was originally developed as a means of encouraging bats for the control of insect pests. Dr Charles Campbell took this to greater extremes early in the 1900s in the construction of huge bat towers to encourage bats for the control of mosquitoes, and hence malaria, in Texas. For hundreds of years, the mining of bat guano for agricultural fertilizer has been important to many communities, and is still today, principally in southeast Asia and in those parts of the tropics where it is carefully controlled.

The role of bats as important pollinators and seed dispersers has also been recognized. They have been used as food, particularly the flying foxes, through much of the Old World tropics, especially on islands where other sources of meat may be limited. They have contributed to medical research in studies of torpor and the preparation of anticoagulants based on the saliva of vampire bats. Bats have also contributed to the war effort: in the American Civil War huge quantities of bat guano were extracted from caves for the production of gunpowder (and this may have caused the first major decline in the now endangered gray bat). Even in the Second World War bats were used in a research project with the object of releasing about one million bats fitted with incendiary devices over major communities in Japan. The bats were expected to fly to buildings where the device would be set off as they entered them. The system might have worked – certainly a bat fitted with such a device did set light to one of the researchers' own laboratories – but, for better or worse, the development of a rival and much more devastating technique condemned the bat project to the archives: the bombing of Hiroshima followed close on the orders to abandon the bat project.

This spectacled flying fox could be regarded as an important contributor to pollination and seed dispersal, as a source of food, or as a pest. Such species can be found in restaurants and markets as food for humans. In some areas they are regarded as pests because they may defoliate their roost trees or because they feed on fruit grown for human consumption. Mostly, these bats feed on fruits that are already too ripe for markets; they may actually have a beneficial function in eating ripe fruit and thereby controlling the insects that invade such fruits. Many important plants that produce fruits, timber and other useful products rely on bats for fertilization and seed dissemination.

Conservation

Population declines of well over 90 per cent in the last 30 or 40 years have been estimated for the Mexican free-tailed bat in North America and for the greater horseshoe bat in Britain. The IUCN Red List of Threatened Animals includes about a quarter of bat species as threatened (e.g. Extinct, Endangered, Vulnerable) and a further quarter as Near Threatened. Ten species are considered extinct, although at the time of writing I hear of the rediscovery of one fruit bat species that had not been seen for over a hundred years – albeit a single specimen found in a market.

The public can enjoy viewing the emergence of Mexican free-tailed bats from caves in New Mexico (above) and Texas (opposite).

The concentration of bat populations into one site makes bat colonies particularly vulnerable. Thus all the females from a vast area may be collected together into a maternity colony in most temperate bats and disturbance to or loss of that one site, can seriously affect the population. Such concentrations may occur all year in the tropics and similar concentrations for hibernation are found in temperate areas. The loss of other less obvious roosts may also be important. The loss of feeding habitat and the regularly used flight lines that offer safe passage between roosts and feeding sites are also threats. Disruption to habitats along migration routes has serious consequences. Over-exploitation of bats for food (fruit bats), rarely for trophies, and increased disturbance by over-exploitation of guano, can lead to serious declines. Ignorance and prejudice can lead to persecution, particularly where there are perceived dangers of the transmission of disease.

As with most animal groups, there are sometimes problems relating to bats. They can be a nuisance in buildings, and there has recently been alarm about diseases that may have their origins in bats. Most of these problems are relatively minor or can be resolved in ways that do not seriously damage bat populations and do not require the rather heavy-handed management that has sometimes been applied without qualified investigation and advice.

Such problems should also be seen in the light of the value of bats in maintaining insect population balance, in pollination and seed dispersal, in guano production (still a vital source of income for some communities), for their part in wider biodiversity and environmental health appreciation, their contribution to medical research, and the interest or even spectacle they provide.

Greater horseshoe bat, a species of conservation concern in Europe.

The development of efforts to bring understanding, both about the myths, e.g. bats get caught in your hair, and about the realities of their behavior, have resulted in a significant swing to interest and concern. That has been particularly so in the last 20 years; it still has a long way to go, but is key to the development of sound conservation. Meanwhile, efforts are made to protect important sites through management agreements, access restrictions and negotiation on works that are likely to affect important bat roosts. Wider habitat protection is more difficult, but it was recognition of the importance of the bats to the island's ecology that led American Samoa to declare a large part of its forests a bat reserve.

Occasionally, populations of a species have reached such a low level in the wild that animals have been taken in to zoos for captive breeding. This has applied to several fruit-bat species, where the species can be maintained as a stock for reintroduction if necessary, and where they can offer valuable educational opportunities.

Common vampire bats can cause economic losses to cattle ranchers and there are occasional outbreaks of attacks on humans. Serious concerns about the effect on non-target species of many efforts at vampire-bat control have led to scientists, vets and human health officials agreeing approved practices, and to international collaboration, which hopefully can be assisted by governments.

The development of appropriate policy and legislation is probably key to the maintenance of healthy bat populations. Bats are protected in many countries, but still classed as vermin in a few. International treaties are encouraging greater concern for the environment and ecology on a world scale. The Convention on International Trade in Endangered Species of Wild Fauna and Flora has restricted the international trade in threatened fruit-bat species (although local exploitation is still not sustainable in some areas). An intergovernmental Agreement on the Conservation of Bats in Europe is developing programs for bat conservation on a pan-European scale in recognition of the fact that bats regularly move across national borders and collaboration is needed between countries for their conservation. A similar arrangement applies between Mexico and the U.S.A. for the protection of migratory species there. And there have been increasing efforts for bat conservationists to collaborate with others to develop good practice; this applies to leisure interests such as caving and tourism, as well as professional interests such as the building industries, forestry and farming.

Progress in conservation requires knowledge of the animals, based on sound survey, monitoring and research. Governments (and others) need encouragement and assistance in protecting their natural heritage. Increasingly, literature and forums such as International Bat Research Conferences and other specialist meetings are addressing bat conservation issues. The IUCN – The World Conservation Union – has a Chiroptera Specialist Group comprising a worldwide network of bat specialists concerned about bat conservation (and regional groups in some areas). IUCN published a conservation action plan for the Old World fruit bats in 1992 that now needs revision. It is currently finalizing an overview action plan for all other bats. Nationally, many countries have developed bat conservation groups or societies, some with a more international remit, such as Bat Conservation International in the U.S.A. or The Bat Conservation Trust in the U.K. Increasingly, they are collaborating in generating action plans for bat conservation locally, nationally and internationally.

Apathy and antipathy have put many bat species at risk, but their profile in conservation initiatives is steadily rising.

Straw-coloured fruit bat eating fruits of musanga, a tree with many constructional uses.

Table of Bat Families

The scientific and common names of species referred to in this book are listed in their appropriate family.

Family Pteropodidae
Cynopterus spp – short-nosed fruit bat
Dyacopterus spadiceus – Dyak fruit bat
Eidolon helvum – straw-coloured fruit bat
Epomophorus spp – epauletted fruit bat
Hypsignathus monstrosus– hammer-headed fruit bat
Nyctimene sp – tube-nosed fruit bat
Pteropus conspicillatus – spectacled flying fox
Pteropus giganteus – Indian flying fox
Rousettus sp – rousette fruit bat
Syconycteris australis – blossom bat

Family Rhinopomatidae
Rhinopoma hardwickii – lesser mouse-tailed bat

Family Craseonycteridae
Craseonycteris thonglongyai – Kitti's hog-nosed bat

Family Emballonuridae
Emballonura semicaudata – Polynesian sheath-tailed bat
Rhynchonycteris naso – proboscis bat
Saccopteryx spp – white-lined sheath-tailed bat

Family Megadermatidae
Lavia frons – yellow bat

Family Rhinolophidae
Rhinolophus ferrumequinum – greater horseshoe bat
Rhinolophus hipposideros – lesser horseshoe bat

Family Noctilionidae
Noctilio leporinus – fisherman bat / bulldog bat

Family Mormoopidae
Pteronotus parnellii – mustached bat

Family Phyllostomidae
Artibeus jamaicensis – Jamaican / greater fruit-eating bat
Centurio senax – wrinkle-faced bat

Desmodus rotundus – common vampire bat
Diaemus youngi – white-winged vampire bat
Diphylla ecaudata – hairy-legged vampire bat
Ectophylla alba – Honduran white bat
Leptonycteris spp – long-nosed bat
Lonchorhina spp – sword-nosed bat
Macrotus californicus – Californian leaf-nosed bat
Phyllostomus hastatus – greater spear-nosed bat
Tonatia spp – round-eared bat
Trachops cirrhosus – frog-eating bat
Uroderma bilobatum – tent-building bat

Family Vespertilionidae
Antrozous pallidus – pallid bat
Corynorhinus spp – big-eared bat
Eptesicus nilssonii – northern bat
Kerivoula spp – woolly bat
Lasiurus borealis – red bat
Lasiurus cinereus – hoary bat
Miniopterus schreibersii – Schreiber's bent-winged bat
Murina spp – tube-nosed bat
Myotis dasycneme – pond bat
Myotis daubentonii – Daubenton's bat
Myotis grisescens – gray bat
Myotis myotis – greater mouse-eared bat
Myotis sodalis – Indiana bat
Myotis spp – mouse-eared bat
Nyctalus noctula – noctule bat
Pipistrellus nathusii – Nathusius's pipistrelle
Pipistrellus pipistrellus – common pipistrelle
Plecotus spp – long-eared bat
Vespertilio murinus – parti-coloured bat

Family Mystacinidae
Mystacina tuberculata – short-tailed bat

Family Molossidae
Otomops martiensseni – African mastiff bat
Tadarida brasiliensis – Mexican free-tailed bat

Bat Facts and Distribution Maps

The 990 or so species of bat are divided into two main groups (suborders).

One group, the Megachiroptera (Old World fruit bats, flying foxes or 'megabats') includes only the single family of about 170 species in the Pteropodidae.

The other group of Microchiroptera ('microbats') includes the other 820 or so species in 17 families.

The following very brief account for each family includes a map of its distribution. Measurements are given as forearm measurement (in / mm); and weight (oz / g).

Pteropodidae

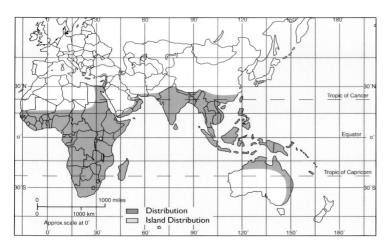

Rhinopomatidae

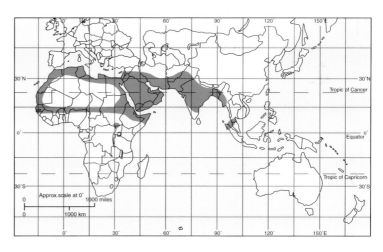

Common name: Old World fruit bats, flying foxes, 'megabats'
Number of species: 41 genera, 170 species
Size: 1½-9 in (35-230 mm), ½ oz-3 lb (15-1500 g)
Diet: fruit, flowers, nectar

Common name: mouse-tailed bat
Number of species: 1 genus, 4 species
Size: 1¾-3 in (45-75 mm), ¼-½ oz (6-14 g)
Diet: insects

Craseonycteridae

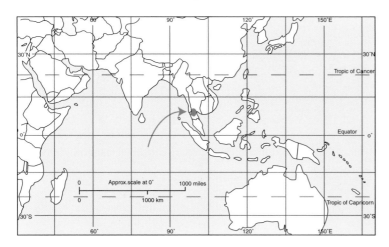

Common name: Kitti's hog-nosed bat
Number of species: 1 genus, 1 species
Size: ¾-1 in (22-26 mm), c ¹⁄₁₆ oz (c 2 g)
Diet: insects

Emballonuridae

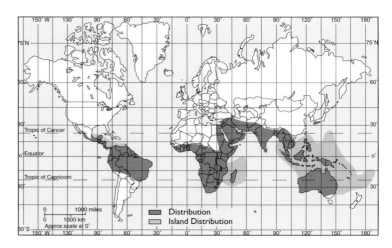

Common name: sheath-tailed bats
Number of species: 13 genera, 48 species
Size: 1½-3¾ in (37-97 mm), ¹⁄₁₆ oz-3½ oz (2-104 g)
Diet: insects

Nycteridae

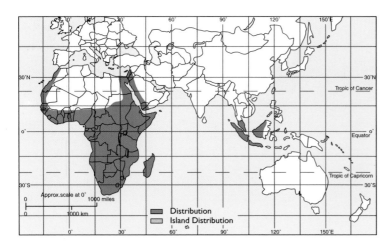

Common name: slit-faced bats
Number of species: 1 genus, 13 species
Size: 1¼-2¼ in (32-60 mm), ⅓ oz-1 oz (10-30 g)
Diet: insects, occasional small vertebrates

Megadermatidae

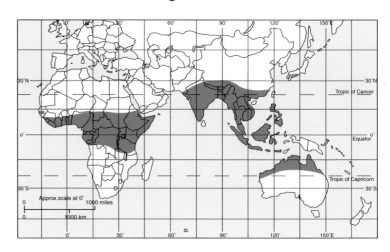

Common name: false vampire bats
Number of species: 4 genera, 5 species
Size: 2-4½ in (50-115 mm), 1-6 oz (25-170 g)
Diet: insects, some small vertebrates

Hipposideridae

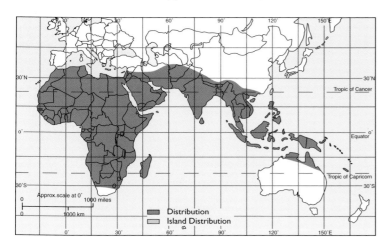

Common name: Old World leaf-nosed bats
Number of species: 9 genera, 73 species
Size: 1-4 in (30-110 mm), ½ oz-6¼ oz (4-180 g)
Diet: insects, occasional small vertebrates

Rhinolophidae

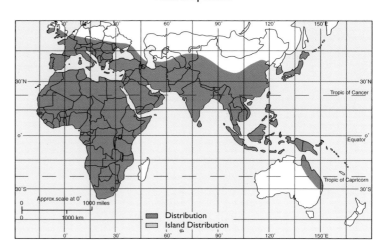

Common name: horseshoe bats
Number of species: 1 genus; 66 species
Size: 1-3 in (30-75 mm); ⅛ oz-1¾ oz (4-50 g)
Diet: insects, occasional small vertebrates

Noctilionidae

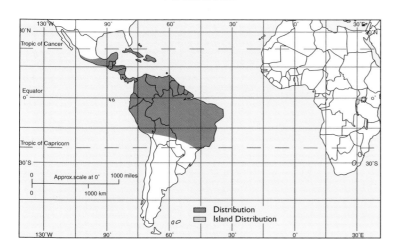

Common name: fisherman bat, bulldog bat
Number of species: 1 genus; 2 species
Size: 2-3½ in (55-90 mm); ½-2¾ oz (18-80 g)
Diet: fish, insects

Mormoopidae

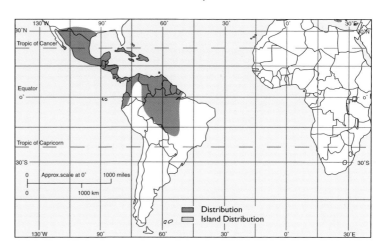

Common name: mustached bat, ghost-faced bat, (naked-backed bat)
Number of species: 2 genera; 8 species
Size: 1¼ in-2½ in (35-65 mm); ¼-¾ oz (7-20 g)
Diet: insects

Phyllostomidae

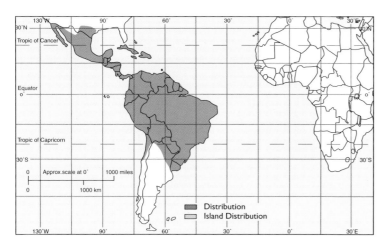

Common name: spear-nosed bats, American leaf-nosed bats
Number of species: 48 genera; 149 species
Size: 1¼-4¼ in (30-110 mm); ⅙ oz-6¾ oz (5-190 g)
Diet: fruit, flowers, nectar, insects, small vertebrates, blood

Natalidae

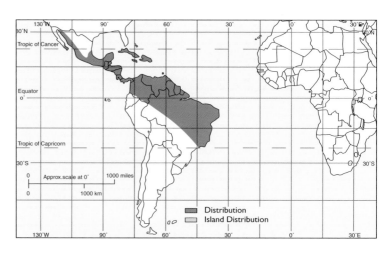

Common name: funnel-eared bat
Number of species: 1 genus, 5 species
Size: 1-1¾ in (27-41 mm); ⅛ oz-⅓ oz (4-10 g)
Diet: insects

Furipteridae

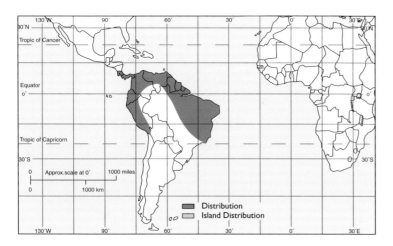

Common name: smoky bat
Number of species: 2 genera; 2 species
Size: 1¼ in-1½ in (30-40 mm); c ⅛ oz (c 3 g)
Diet: insects

Thyropteridae

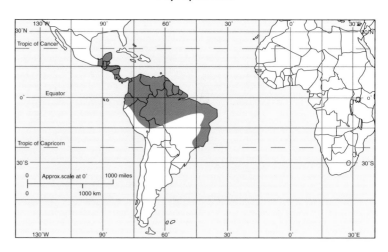

Common name: disc-winged bat
Number of species: 1 genus; 3 species
Size: 1-1½ in (27-38 mm); ½-⅙ oz (4-5 g)
Diet: insects

Myzopodidae

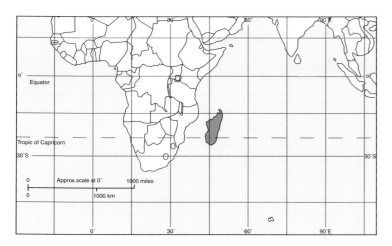

Common name: sucker-footed bat
Number of species: 1 genus, 1 species
Size: 1¾ in-2 in (46-50 mm); ¼-⅓ oz (8-10 g)
Diet: insects

Vespertilionidae

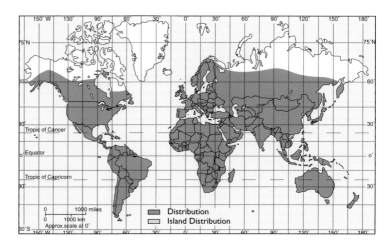

Common name: plain-nosed, vesper bats
Number of species: 37 genera; 348 species
Size: 1-3 in (22-75 mm); ⅛ oz-2 oz (4-50 g)
Diet: insects

Mystacinidae

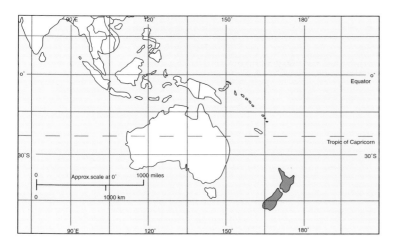

Common name: New Zealand short-tailed bat
Number of species: 1 genus; 1 species
Size: 1½-1¾ in (40-45 mm); c ½ oz (12-15 g)
Diet: insects, flowers

Molossidae

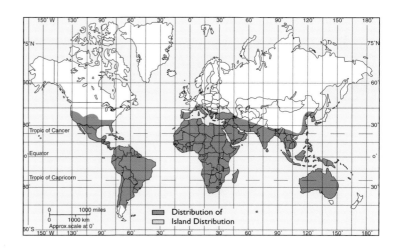

Common name: free-tailed bat, mastiff bat
Number of species: 12 genera; 87 species
Size: 1-3¼ in (27-85 mm); ¼-3½ oz (5-100 g)
Diet: insects

Index

*Entries in **bold** indicate pictures*

Biographical Note

Tony Hutson has been a fan of bats since he was just 10 years old. He was the Bat Project Officer for the Fauna and Flora Preservation Society from 1984-87, and is currently a conservation adviser to the Bat Conservation Trust. He was the editor of *Bat News* from 1984 to 1998. He has traveled widely in Central and South America, Africa, Europe, Australia, and the Indian Ocean, where he encountered his first flying fox in 1968.

Recommended Reading

Altringham, J.D. 1996. *Bats - Biology and Behaviour*. Oxford University Press, Oxford / New York / Tokyo.

Hill, J.E. & Smith, J.D. 1984. *Bats - A Natural History*. British Museum (Natural History), London.

Hutson, A.M., Mickleburgh, S.P. & Racey, P.A. (in press). 'Global Action Plan for Microchiropteran Bats'. IUCN, Gland.

Kunz, T.H. 1988. *Ecological and Behavioral Methods for the Study of Bats*. Smithsonian Institution Press, Washington.

Mickleburgh, S.P., Hutson, A.M. & Racey, P.A. 1992. 'Old World Fruit Bats – An Action Plan for their Conservation'. IUCN, Gland.

Nowak, R.M. 1994. *Walker's Bats of the World*. The John Hopkins University Press, Baltimore & London.

Wilson, D.E. 1997. *Bats in Question – The Smithsonian Answer Book*. Smithsonian Institution Press, Washington / London.